by Lee Priestley
illustrations by

Marquita Peterson

Yucca Tree Press

Yucca Tree Press, 2130 Hixon Drive, Las Cruces, New Mexico 88005-3305.

First Printing May 1996

Library of Congress Cataloging in Publication Data.

Priestley, Lee

WITHIN SOUND OF THE BUGLE

1. Southwestern Frontier Forts–Fiction.
I. Lee Priestley. II. Title

Library of Congress Catalog Card Number: 95-061958

ISBN: 1-881325-18-0

Illustrations by Marquita Peterson

So especially for Sergeant Daniel Newton Jones, 82nd Battalion, Horse-drawn Field Artillery, USA, who has lived years of 'Hear-say History.'

Editor's Note

Lee Priestley's delightful collection of 'Hearsay History' presents another perspective on how life was lived at frontier forts during New Mexico's Territorial period. The stories are not necessarily in chronological order.

TABLE OF CONTENTS

Foreword

Dim trails over mesa and mountain, down dry arroyos or splashing through shallow river crossings lead to traces of foundations or crumbling walls, the silent survivors of the forts that held the frontiers.

Many of these southwestern forts persist only as names on old maps or in War Department records and the tales they can tell await the research of historians and fascinated amateurs. The stories given here, still lively despite more than a hundred years' burial under official records and reports, are no more significant than a hundred more that can be brought to light.

What life was like under the flags of the frontier can be glimpsed in the fallible memories and "informed speculation" that can occasionally be found among the facts and the footnotes. Add unofficial viewpoints to approximate what really happened.

Army life was hard for enlisted men, volunteers and officers. Duty could lead to death; monotony could crescendo into massacre. The bare essentials of life were achieved only by great and unending effort.

Security? That could be only a word depending upon many factors beyond control of crowding together for safety. It also increased the rub and clash of personality that often led to violence. Lack of privacy could be painful. Off duty was restricted by the order that "all personnel must be, at all times, within the sound of the bugle."

Shelter, as a part of security, was seldom complete. The fort roof often leaked or collapsed. On the march, a uniform – usually unsuitable for climate or weather – a bed roll and half of a shelter tent were scarcely luxury.

Food? On the frontier each trooper was reminded often that he was expendable; his horse was not. Therefore, the mounts that carried the men, the pack animals and the teams that freighted their every essential were fed first. Providing forage and fodder was a never-ending duty. Then the trooper could eat. His fare was commonly the ubiquitous beans and bacon varied with whatever ingenuity could add. At the forts, small garden plots, solicitously tended, provided greens and onions and the occasional tomato and rare potato.

What was left, given all the negatives? No trooper named them but they lived devotion to duty, loyalty to a cause, comradeship and compassion, heroism and bravery. The men would have jeered at such "high falutin' ideas" even while they lived by them. Strong language and rough jokes lightened the labor and the hardships that secured the western expansion of a nation.

What may one call these episodes? Perhaps historical fiction comes closest. Firmly based on history, told about actual people (some appearing under their real names), they lived these events. Perhaps their viewpoints may record truth more faithfully than many official facts.

And all "within the sound of the bugle."

Quiet Day at Fort Selden

Lieutenant James Haskell, 9th Cavalry, U.S. Army assigned to Fort Selden, Territory of New Mexico paced on the porch of his bachelor's quarters as he waited impatiently for the mailman.

He surveyed the view before him without enthusiasm. He supposed it was a fine prospect if you liked dusty empty miles.

The shallow water of the ford on the Rio Grande gleamed placidly under the sun that had faded the land to a thousand shades of tan and brown and bronze green. To the west and south, the perfect cone of Picacho Peak rose against the sky. Farther on the horizon the triple mountains named 'The Three Sisters' faded into blue distance.

Fort Selden had to be the most godawful duty in the southwest, probably in the entire western world. Silence and space and plenty of it.

The fort hadn't always been this mixture of one part massacre to five hundred parts of monotony. (A conscientious soldier, the Lieutenant had learned the history of his past.) From earliest days, travelers had come here to the only shallow rock-bottom, quicksand-free river crossing for miles. The fort gave protection to the wagons coming from Santa Fe or up from Chihuahua on the eighty dangerous, waterless miles of the *Jornada del Muerto*, the 'Dead Man's Trail.'

As far back as 1772 soldiers chased away "brigands of Spanish descent" – notably one Chali Navarro – and kept a respectful distance from the Indians who came from all over the southwest to bathe their aches and pains in the hot springs which were less than a mile from the fort.

Don Juan de Oñate's ponderous mass of colonists passed over the ford leaving one of the number behind in a lonely grave. Pedro Robledo gave his name to the mountain rising over the sparkling water.

Three governments in turn, the Spanish-Mexican, Confederate, and the United States recognized its strategic importance. Early in the War Between the States, Confederate Captain B. Coopwood had set up a recruiting post there with a scouting detail to spy out the Union forts to the north. When the reports were encouraging, Colonel H. H. Sibley marched and fought over the *Sangre de Cristo* Mountains to Santa Fe, aiming at Fort Union. He was turned back decisively at Glorieta Pass in March 1862. Then the fort on the Rio Grande was named to honor Union Colonel Henry R. Selden who had fought against Sibley from the *Jornada* to Glorieta.

That brought the Lieutenant to the present and the tedium of this post. Lord, Lord, the endless days! It wasn't the work, it was the boredom. His farthest excursion was to the top of Robledo to work the shutters of the heliograph that blinked messages to other forts. The greatest excitement was a noisy quarrel between a cook and the mess sergeant over too little tomato in the soup.

The Army did its best to keep them busy with fiddling routines, while sternly ordering them to stay away from the gamblers and the girls. Captain MacArthur brought in a pool table and books and organized ball teams. That helped. But mostly the hours stretched endless and empty – empty as the landscape.

When he looked out to the ford he saw the water wagon returning loaded with sloshing barrels. The Lieutenant grinned, sharing his Buffalo Soldiers' pleasure in their favorite release from monotony. The flash of red between the two troopers was surely the headband on the Captain's precocious second son. Young Douglas tied his hair back like an Indian, and refused to wear a shirt or shoes; he was the pet of the Post and the despair of Pinkey, his mother.

The Lieutenant admonished himself hastily. He must never, even in his private thoughts, refer to the Captain's wife as other than "Mrs. MacArthur, Ma'am." As the daughter of the aristocratic Pinckney family of the deep South, a nickname was unforgivable.

He grinned, watching the wagon come sailing along. He knew his troopers bargained for the water wagon duty and a chance to spoil the Captain's younger son. Brat though he was, he livened the Post, his antics breaking the monotony of the empty days. When he and his brother raced lizards they couldn't be blamed if the troopers gambled on the results, could they?

Still, he told himself, empty days were better. Better to have no train of *paisanos* creeping fearfully toward Point of Rocks hoping the rasp of wooden wheels against wooden axles would somehow escape hidden ears. Better than fool-hardy ranchers searching for strayed or stolen stock. If the *Jornada* was not empty, a rescue detail must be sent out, usually too late to save the men or recover the animals, particularly the horses.

The Lieutenant, trained to the Cavalry's edict that men were expendable but horses were not, winced while thinking of the way stolen animals were wasted. Native-owned horses had little bottom to begin with, being haphazardly fed. When raided by a dozen methods (some mightily clever, he conceded) they were driven hard to get away, starved on a few bites of scarce grass, then if – no, *when* – they went down were slaughtered and eaten half raw. The big gut filled with water and wrapped around a living horse provided the next day's stinking necessity. Mules didn't get that far, for Indians preferred their meat.

Aside from their cruelty to man and animals, the Lieutenant knew a grudging admiration for the savage cavalry he occasionally encountered. (The hardest fighting of the Indian Wars was over.) He understood how narrowly they lived between death and starvation. He could see them, most times, as a people with a right to live in their barren homeland. He knew he was almost alone in that viewpoint for most soldiers and citizens considered Apaches to be noxious predators best speedily exterminated.

He prowled restlessly on his narrow porch. The mail came at different times every week. That was one way José Turietta, the mailman, hoped to elude the Indians. The poor fellow saw an ambush behind every mesquite, and who could blame him? He'd several times been chased to the gates of the fort.

One of the mailman's stratagems had been to muffle his horses' hooves with tied-on sacking. That made the black troopers jeer. They were not too pleased when the postman called them 'Buffalo Soldiers,' a name picked up from the Indians who said the trooper's black skin and curly hair were like the buffalo.

"That scaredy-cat Mex thinks he gonna fool any Apaches by makin' his horse go 'thump, thump, thump' instead of 'Clatter! Clatter! Clatter!' he's the fool!" Hooting and slapping their knees, they had the last laugh.

The water wagon had drawn closer so the Lieutenant saw that the Captain's son, standing between the two troopers, proudly drove the mule himself. As he made that observation, he heard the boy whoop and begin to slash the mule with the ends of the lines.

The startled animal broke into a lumbering gallop. The water wagon, sloshing barrels, yelling boy and laughing troopers cheering him on, careened through the gate, nearly over-running the sentry who had opened for them.

The Lieutenant closed his eyes and prayed that Pinkey – "Mrs. MacArthur, Ma'am" wasn't within sight or sound. She would blame the black troopers for encouraging her son and the Lieutenant for not controlling the troopers. It would turn out to be James Haskell's fault. Didn't he remember he was unofficially charged to keep an eye on Douglas?

How he could do that if he had as many eyes as a sprouted potato wasn't clear. Take the case of the button-up shoes. Pinkey – "Mrs. MacArthur, Ma'am," tried to make a "little gentleman" of her younger son. When she persuaded him to wear a shirt as the Post stood Retreat, she had felt victorious. So she next tried to get Douglas' feet into shoes. Had she provided cowboy boots or even moccasins, she might have had temporary success, but button-up shoes?

His tantrum, loud and long, ended with the boy throwing the despised footwear down the privy. That convenience, commodious and newly built, plastered inside and out, was the Captain's pride. What he said or did at the manner of the privy's christening, the Lieutenant did not care to know. The Captain's son, to his mother's despair, remained defiantly barefooted.

The Lieutenant saw that he didn't need to worry about the troopers, soaked and entangled with the water barrels or the sentry's near escape from being run down. The men were laughing and telling Douglas what a great driver he was. The boy was the pet of the Post, encouraged in his bratishness by the whole strength. The Lieutenant found himself grinning, too.

Then he went back to his own affairs. Where *was* the mail? He wanted to send some money – not much on Uncle Sam's pay for chasing Indians – to the Louisiana Lottery in hope of getting lucky. Winning was about as likely as being struck by lightning, he knew, but it helped to pass the time. The Captain discouraged serious gambling on post.

The mail might bring a letter from Liz who was taking her time answering his proposal that she come West to marry him. He had told her that the time was right since a quarters was available now that the wife of the Infantry Company commander had gone screaming mad and had been shipped back home. He was not really hopeful that Liz, a desk general's daughter, would exchange Washington where she danced holes in her shoes for this dull place.

He remember that one of Pinkey's predecessors – he *must* say, "Mrs. MacArthur, Ma'am" – had called For Selden "a quite unattractive place" that she had left without shedding tears.

He surveyed the "unattractive place." Barracks for two companies, one infantry, one cavalry, officers' quarters, mess halls, kitchens, bakery, commissary, ten-bed hospital, guard house, stables and corrals for sixteen horses and a few other addments clustered around or stretched beside the Parade. It all looked better, now that the new-planted trees had leafed out to give some welcome shade. But he had to agree with the sniffing predecessor's judgment, "quite unattractive."

His bachelor quarters were equally spare. The narrow porch where he paced was roofed with cottonwood poles and brush, the home for assorted inspects that came down to sleep in his boots. The square adobe room behind the porch crowded together his camp bed, a chair and a table that doubled as a desk and washstand, with a tin basin and pitcher to serve one function. A length of calico across a corner protected his dress uniform and his side arms when they weren't on him. The hostiles were quiet but even Pinkey – oh, forget it! wore a pistol.

At last the mailman – he started as José Turietta rounded the base of Robledo Peak in a cloud of dust and pounded through the ford whipping his horse, impeded with the sacking mufflers, to a frantic speed.

"What the devil is he running from?" the Lieutenant asked himself. Then he saw another cloud of dust at the curve. Indians! Four, maybe five, chasing the mailman. Indians?

He ran for the gate, yelling at the sentry, leisurely closing as he laughed with the troopers and the boy.

"Open up! Let the mail in!"

The Indians, coming up fast were, strangely, struggling to control their mounts. Bolting? Runaways? Rearing? "What the devil could make an Indian lose control of his horse?"

They were charging the gate!

"Close it!" the Lieutenant yelled. "After the mailman's in, you dunderheads!"

"You just said to open it, sir." The sentry was aggrieved. "If the Lieutenant would make up his mind – "

The Indians, fighting their frantic ponies, poured through the gate on the heels of the mailman, scattering like seeds from a burst pod. They wrenched their ponies around trying to head back for the gate and over-ran Turietta.

"Open the gate!" the Lieutenant yelled. "Let 'em out! Move, man! Shove! Shove, you worthless – "

"Open! Shut! Shove! Man don't know what he wants," the water wagon trooper grumbled, moving languidly.

The Lieutenant's yell stuck in his throat, his feet wouldn't move, his eyes refused to believe what they saw.

A camel!

Out of the dust cloud, loping hopefully, came a camel! Impossibly, a camel!

The troopers froze. The boy climbed the Lieutenant's leg.

"What that thing?" the sentry whispered.

"Lord Almighty, it gonna eat us!"

"Lemme outa here – "

Douglas was braver. Clinging to the Lieutenant's yellow-stripped leg he looked again. "I saw a picture – it's a camel! What's it doing here?"

What a camel was doing at Fort Selden, Territory of New Mexico raced through the Lieutenant's mind. When Jefferson Davis served as Secretary of the Army in 1850, he had imported camels for experimental use as beasts of burden on the desert southwest. The experiment proved successful beyond hopes. The camels could carry heavier loads, travel farther and faster on less feed and water than horses or mules.

Then two problems arose, the first concerned the camel's feet. The Arabian deserts of their homeland were largely sand. Most of the so-called "Great American Desert" was rough and stony. The surfaces bruised and cut the camel's feet. The second and unsolvable problem was the camel's smell. The horses and mules and their handlers found the sight and smell – the awful stink – of the camels intolerable. When excited, the foreign creatures chased and showered the other animals with odorous spit. Stampedes, wrecked wagons, scattered merchandise and infuriated teamsters stretched from Texas to California.

When no solution was found, the camels were sold to zoos and circuses, then the remnant was turned out to survive as possible. Here was one of the survivors, lonely, looking for companionship. Probably raised in a Bedouin tent like a member of the family, the Lieutenant thought. No wonder the camel wanted company.

"Close the gate!" he yelled. "Damn it! Close! Close –"

The camel, spitting and whistling in wild excitement trampled the sentry and scattered Indians and ponies, crashed into the corral fence and charged the troopers brought out by the noise.

The Parade swarmed like a stirred-up ant hill. The full strength variously pulled Indians off ponies and chased horses rocketing in every direction. Pinkey's bossy cow mooing and kicking up her heels met the camel face to face.

"Oh, Lord, there goes our milk and butter!" the Lieutenant groaned. Turning, the mail bag swatted him as Turietta's horse bucked and tangled his legs in the sacking and fell across the Lieutenant's legs.

Dazed, and with a throbbing lump the size of an egg on his head, the Lieutenant sat in a puddle that smelled as bad as the spit running down his neck and stared at the burst mail bag. Maybe he had some letters. None from Liz – call it a pocket veto. One from his brother who was proud of "his service at the dangerous post." The Lieutenant snorted. More troopers were lost in those dens of iniquity in Leasburg than ever saw an Apache. A letter from his mother anxious about his safety; one from a friend complaining about the hardships of his Washington desk job. That left the *Rio Grande Republican.*

He glanced over the weekly with wavering attention until he saw a heading sandwiched between notice of a bazaar at Loretto Academy and a police threat that stray burros would be impounded.

"Visitors from the Fort"

Sergeant Patrick O'Neil and a picked squad are enjoying ten days in well-earned relaxation at the Amador Hotel.

They occupy rooms Carmen, Lupita, Soledad and Maria and are said to be enjoying the favors of those *senoritas.* The squad has been handsomely entertained in La Mesilla, we are told.

Beats chasing Apaches, doesn't it, boys?

The Lieutenant swore enviously. Pat O'Neil and that "picked squad" had ridden out with ten day's rations in pursuit of raiders who had burned a ranch house near San Augustin Pass. He couldn't fault Pat much. Who wanted to chase hostiles who could disappear in the sand before your eyes when you could guzzle a gallon of Mesilla wine and tumble a willing girl?

He thought vaguely that the riot must have subsided, for the sentry and the water wagon troopers having caught up Pinkey's – oops, Mrs. MacArthur Ma'am's, cow stood by him watching. In a ragged, agitated column, Indians and half the livestock in the valley raced away ahead of the determined camel, and splashed through the ford.

"Ten to one, that parade will cross the border before sundown," the sentry said.

James Haskell tore open his letter to the Louisiana Lottery and extracted his ten peso note. "I'll take you up on that," Trooper."

A dirty and furious small boy rose up in the Lieutenant's face and snatched the ten pesos. "Gimme that! You know my papa don't allow you guys to gamble! And I'm going to *get you*! You scared my camel away! He was hungry I bet, and lonesome and you let him get away. I wanted to keep him for a pet! When my papa comes home I'm going to have him *get you*!"

Lieutenant James Haskell, 9th Cavalry, U.S. Army posted to Fort Selden, Territory of New Mexico thought about getting lucky. He caught up and hugged the clamoring boy, and waited for the lightning to strike.

The Major Led with Magnificent Indifference

Trooper Patrick Ryan, 3rd U.S. Cavalry kept stumbling as he walked his post at Fort Fillmore, New Mexico Territory, because he looked at the stars more than he watched his feet.

His two-hour sentry go didn't make a difference to these bright distant worlds; to Paddy Ryan's tired feet in too-tight boots, time stood still. Surely he was due to be relieved soon. He heard something, a small cautious sound. The corral gate creaked. Advancing, his rifle at the ready he challenged, "Who goes there?"

The night silence was unbroken. Paddy thought uneasily that he might have used the wrong words. Recruited a few weeks ago, he had been told plenty how ignorant he was. He tried again.

"Halt! or I'll shoot!"

Those were the right words. The corral gate swept Paddy back into the fence – yelling mixed with pounding hooves. The horses disappeared into the darkness. Paddy's shot banged uselessly at the indifferent stars.

The barracks turned out in shouting and confusion. The empty corral verified that forty horses were gone. The men readied for a command to pursue the thieves. The command didn't come. Perplexed, the troopers finally went back to their beds. Late in the morning someone ventured to ask the Commandant, Major Lynde, about the lack of interest in the loss of the horses. A brusque opinion, that the matter was of no importance since the thieves from El Paso couldn't be identified, ended the conversation.

As he went about his duties, Trooper Ryan thought about the fix he had gotten himself into. He had joined the army back home in Massachusetts after a fiery abolitionist orator convinced him that he should help free the African slaves from plantations in the South.

Since then he had been moved from here to there (very uncomfortably) to be stationed in a strange place that had no connection he could see with freeing anyone.

He had learned a little about his station. Fort Fillmore, named to honor President James Fillmore, had been founded in 1851 by Lieutenant S. D. Miles on land leased from Hugh Stevenson of El Paso, Texas.

The men came from Doña Ana and Las Cruces, where they had been garrisoned long enough to wear out their welcome. The villagers, glad of the soldiers' protection when Indians constantly threatened, were equally pleased when soldiers were no longer billeted in their houses. Food supplies and pretty daughters were no longer at risk.

Troops came to Fort Fillmore when Fort Thorn was abandoned. That hard luck post, unwisely built in a swampy, often-flooded area was often incapacitated when most of the troopers were down with fever and chills. The men, their arms and all supplies strengthened Fort Fillmore.

Now, in 1861, the fort had grown into clustered adobe houses and corrals that sheltered seven hundred troopers, one hundred women and children and various numbers of livestock, minus the forty horses stolen in the night. Indians were said to lurk everywhere but he hadn't seen any.

Paddy supposed these hundreds of men were stationed here because the top brass wanted to hold this wild far land for the Union. He listened to the troopers; they usually knew the reason. The Commandant and most of his officers talked loyalty to the Union, the men said, but actually were southern sympathizers.

"'Galvanized Yankees!'" the troopers joked. They were familiar with a process for treating metal that changed the basic gray color to blue. They said many of the officers wearing blue uniforms were only waiting for the right time to resign their commissions in the Union Army and then join the Rebs.

Trooper Ryan wanted to believe that his commander was loyal to the flag under which he served. But there was the matter of forty horses given, in effect, to some enemy. As a cavalryman, he had been impressed that men were expendable but horses were not.

He still puzzled two weeks later. The fort went on alert when news came that Lieutenant Colonel John R. Baylor of the Confederate Army had captured Fort Bliss, Texas in July. Within the month, the Texans had advanced into New Mexico Territory and easily occupied La Mesilla.

When the Major learned that the Confederates were firmly established on the Plaza there, less than ten miles from Fort Fillmore, he finally moved. Taking four hundred and eighty men (Trooper Paddy Ryan among them) he advanced cautiously until within shouting distance of the village, then halted without mounting an attack.

Trooper Ryan, dismounted as commanded, grew increasingly uneasy. Why? A wagon load of whys. They matched or outnumbered the Rebs. He wasn't trained in strategy but surely the Major had been, but now he had given up the advantages of darkness and surprise.

He squirmed to ease a foot, damn the too-tight boots, and found he had a neighbor. He apologized in a whisper to his

Captain, C. H. McNally, whom he admired for his outspoken loyalty to his uniform. He ventured a question.

"Sir, what do you think we can expect?"

The sound the Captain made was hopeless. "The dear Lord may know." He laughed without amusement, "Not the Major. He leads with magnificent indifference. We're to move forward to spy out the situation. When we contact the Texans, the Major will move up and support us."

The stars told Trooper Ryan that dawn was near. The small wind that stirs before sunrise rustled the leaves of the cornfield that bordered the village. Peering into the half light they saw faint movement along the rows. Baylor's men waited in the protection of the tall corn and the banks of the canal.

The Captain ordered the four twelve-pounder mountain howitzers into firing position. The troopers sprang to attention.

"We'll give them a couple of rounds," the Captain told the troopers. "We won't do much damage – we don't have the fire power, but we'll let them know we're here and signal the Major to move up to support us.

The sun cleared the spires of the Organ Mountains. The light colored the western peaks with rose and gold. The Captain gave the order, "Fire!"

The howitzers banged and whistled as the shells fell severally into the cornfield or splashed in the canal. A rattle of small arms made a ragged reply.

"We'll give the Major a few minutes to catch up," the Captain said.

They waited.

The silence grew long. The light grew brighter. The rustling in the cornfield moved closer.

Finally the Captain said cheerfully, "Looks like we'll have the honor of taking La Mesilla by ourselves." He nodded at two troopers. "Hold the horses. We'll make smaller targets afoot. No glorious charge of the Light Brigade for us. Advance! Fire at will!"

Hopeless. Trooper Ryan knew it would be hopeless. Eighteen men and one officer, however recklessly brave, could not take a village. They got off four volleys before a shot from the Texans knocked the Captain's pistol from his hand. A second shot wounded him seriously.

Paddy Ryan caught the sagging weight of the Captain. "Somebody give me a hand! Get him up on my horse, then get the hell out of here!"

Struggling to stay on his horse, held to a plod, to keep the Captain from falling off while he jammed his hat against the bleeding wound in the Captain's side, they trailed far behind the rest of the detail. It was the last straw for Paddy Ryan to be challenged by a sentry.

He didn't so much dismount as fall off trying to protect the fainting Captain. "A half-dead hero and a mad-as-hell trooper reporting."

The Captain in the hospital and out of danger, Paddy Ryan tried to report. He faced the Major who sat at his desk red-faced and glassy-eyed. When it became clear that the man neither knew nor cared why a blood-stained, exhausted trooper stood there, Paddy Ryan saluted and went away.

Orders were given sometime by someone. The alert was maintained while the fort was readied to withstand assault. The corrals were strengthened by a wall of hay bales; buildings added inside shutters for windows and reinforcements for doors. Food was stockpiled; the water supply secured. The post doctor, responsible for the hospital and medical supplies, got ready for possible casualties. Weaponry from cannon to side-arms, disposed to best advantage and made available, finished the feverish preparations. The fort could stand assault.

On the hottest day of that summer, the Post collectively sat down, having done its duty. The fort was secure. No enemy approached; no savages lurked –

The Major slammed out of Headquarters. Lurching over to the row of whiskey barrels, he yelled for assembly. Before the startled men had entirely arrived, he gave his orders.

"Abandon fort! At *once*!"

"At once!" Paddy Ryan, along with the other men and officers stood in stunned, disbelieving silence. Then the shouted questions pelted the Major like thrown rocks.

"Why? What for? Why? *Why? Why?*

The Major, red-faced and roaring, brandished a pistol. "Because I say so! I'm your commanding officer and I give the orders here! I'll shoot any bastard that disobeys me!"

Paddy Ryan thought the Major might carry out his threat. Drunk he was, and maybe mad besides. He could see his thoughts reflected in the faces of the others. And, the Major was the commanding officer. Maybe he knew something the troopers didn't.

The Major's orders became less belligerent, if still incomprehensible. "I want every man ready to march by full dark. Cooler then. We'll travel fast and light to San Augustin Springs, then continue for Fort Stanton."

He stopped to chuckle. "We'll play a good joke on the boys from Texas. Destroy anything they could use. We'll leave them an empty fort and nobody to capture. We'll march as ready and form up farther down the trail." Two days rations and two canteens per man. Don't want to be thirsty."

The Major stopped giving orders and began to laugh uproariously. He holstered his pistol with some fumbling and picked up a hand ax. He smashed in the head of the first whiskey barrel.

"Every bastard come past me here. I'll fill one canteen – two if you want. Can't let the damn Texans guzzle our rot gut."

Begun in confusion, the evacuation proceeded in chaos. Ordered to destroy stocked supplies and burn the buildings, the troopers made a show of following the Major's conflicting orders. Token fires were set, then extinguished; a few sacks of flour slashed open were flung to the floor. The rest was left to fall into the hands of the Texans.

At one o'clock in the morning in rank disorder, with no discernible plans, the evacuation began. Slipping back after his canteen was filled with the mandatory whiskey, Trooper Ryan dumped the liquor, refilled the canteen with water and found another. He ran to the hospital where Captain McNally and three other wounded or disabled men were being left with food and water.

"Goody-by for now, Sir," he said, saluting. "You'll be easy here until the Texans come. They'll take better care of you than you've had. Anyway, I'll be back soon."

The Captain said anxiously, "The Major said you will head for Fort Stanton? That's a long march."

"Don't worry, sir. We'll never see Fort Stanton."

Paddy Ryan's prophecy was self-fulfilling. The heat next day exhausted both men and their water supply. Six miles from the Springs the suffering horses began to give out.

Decisive for once, the Major took the strongest horses and a small group of troopers to ride ahead and come back with water.

"Come back?" Paddy Ryan said scornfully. "Don't look for him."

Chosen for the detail, he gathered all the empty canteens he could carry and made others do likewise. "If you want to get out of this alive," he said.

The Springs, at an August low, couldn't provide enough water. Taking what they could, the detail started back to the staggering troopers. Scarcely turned around, the Major felt the ride back would be too much for him. He elected to stay at the Springs and wait for the Command to come up. Speechless, the detail went back.

By rest and the strictest rationing, the command made it to the Springs. But the rear guard had seen Texans approaching close enough to count.

The Major (this according to his official report later) sounded the Call to Arms and was dismayed to find only one hundred men able to respond. He promptly ordered them to surrender.

The officers, even though they had southern sympathies, protested with violent shoutings. The words "treachery" and "dishonor" were heard.

The Major brandished his pistols again. "I'm your commander!" he shouted. "What I say goes and don't you bastards forget it. Shut up! You're all under arrest."

His eyes fell on Trooper Ryan. "Corporal!"

"Golly!" Paddy thought. "I just got promoted."

Guns waving, the Major yelled, "I'm surrendering Fort Fillmore! If any of you bastards question my decision, I'll shoot you on the spot!"

"Trooper," the Major found Paddy Ryan again.

"There goes my promotion," Paddy thought.

"Trooper, take a detail and contact the Texans."

With "magnificent indifference" Major surrendered a garrison of seven hundred trained and equipped men to less than two hundred and fifty Confederates, haphazardly armed and almost untrained without firing a shot.

Correction: one shot was heard. The Major's brandished pistol went off with a bang.

"All I've got to say," Trooper Paddy Ryan muttered, "this is a hell of a way to free the slaves."

The Burros' Revenge

Private Mike Murphy, raising the earthworks at Fort Craig, that year of 1862, threw a shovel full of dirt behind him. The wind blew most of it back over his head and blinded his eyes.

When he stepped backward, the loose fill at the base of the ten-foot wall dumped him into the ditch. He landed on something wiggling and lumpy and cursed the day he had come.

Actually, Fort Craig, on a mesa gently sloping down to the western bank of the Rio Grande, was the best of the military installations in New Mexico Territory. Founded in 1853 at the northern end of the *Jornada del Muerto*, the dreaded waterless, Indian-dominated *Camino Real* linked Chihuahua in Mexico with Santa Fe, gateway to the United States. South-bound travelers inched along to Fort Selden and the fertile green Mesilla Valley.

Private Murphy found no fault with the site of Fort Craig; it was the dust and the duty and the discipline that irked him. He blamed the dust most of all. Dust rising around the hooves and wheels of the travelers fearfully crossing the *Jornada del Muerto* betrayed them to the Apache. Dust shrouded the details sent to escort and patrols sent to survey the trail down to greener lands.

Private Murphy blamed the dust for his personal problems. Dust rose on the wind and then settled on every surface of a thirsty land. Water was scarce, but whiskey was plentiful. Enlisted men and officers became heavy drinkers according to their opportunities.

Wasn't it unfair, Private Murphy asked himself, that only troopers went to the guardhouse for taking a few too many? During his frequent sojourns there he had seen no officers.

Squirming to ease his back from whatever was under him, he thought one might expect that officers who were notoriously hard drinkers would go a little easy on an enlisted man who had taken a few too many. But not the Colonel. He'd clap you back in the guardhouse if you walked past the sutler's whiskey barrels.

Maybe even put a man in the dungeons. Private Murphy didn't know or want to know what awful offense would send a man into them. He had looked fearfully down a stair leading to cells too small to stand up in or lay down stretched out. No one down there now. When Colonel Canby learned that Confederate volunteers led by General Henry Sibley had marched from Fort Bliss, Texas to New Mexico Territory at La Mesilla, he had set every man jack, soldier and civilian alike (and all the Mexican villagers he could catch), to working on the fortifications. There must be a thousand men wearing blisters on their hands getting ready for the Rebs who threatened Fort Craig.

This fall into the ditch beside the earthen wall must have knocked him a little silly for he heard a voice and felt a wiggle underneath.

" ... *por favor, Señor*," the voice said faintly.

"Lord save us, what are you doing down here?" Rolling and squirming, Private Murphy rolled off a small cringing Mexican who had to be one of the fort's native neighbors. "Have I killed you then, *hombre? Como se llama?*"

Private Murphy liked the scared men the Colonel had rounded up and made to work without pay. The Irish and the

Spanish now got along well and the days when the great armada shipwrecked itself on the rocky coast of the old country were long past. He had enough of their musical lingo to talk with them *pequeño*, a little.

His companion in the ditch named himself as Juan Garcia and he lived fairly close to the fort. Mike then felt another movement at his back, then a nuzzle, and finally a puff of hay-sweet breath. Sure, the ditch was getting crowded. Juan Garcia made anxious shooing motions at the two burros. "*Avanti, avanti, mis amigos*." He introduced them further as, "*Mis viejos,* my old ones."

Why they were in the ditch took considerable jabber. Juan wasn't being paid so he had no money to buy fodder for *los viejos* from the fort sutler. Since he had no time, he couldn't take the old burros out to forage. The sutler had stripped the nearby mesa for everything he could sell under his contract to provision the fort's livestock. *Mis amigos* were existing on sticks and straws.

Nothing between the rough hides and a rack of bones – starving they were, man and beast, while the sutler lined his pockets as "forage agent for the government." Mike told himself an Irishman could get the best of a sticky fingered Federal any day. He said to Juan, "Sarge will be coming to run me back to the guardhouse and you'd better scamper, but first, look here."

With a stick he drew a line or two on the ground to map the middle of the north earthworks not yet finished. "There's a window in the guardhouse about here. You'll see some light. Take *los viejos* and wait in the shadow. I'll have something for you."

Sarge was hot and sore. "Get on with you – " he described Private Murphy in a few cuss words. "While you lean on a shovel in the shade I've been on the top of the wall bustin' my ass rigging up pretend cannon." He laughed and spoke disrespectfully of the commanding general of the Confederate forces threatening For Craig from the east side of the river. "When old soak Sibley sees these cottonwood logs he will think everyone is a cannon aimed right down his throat."

Mike Murphy fingered the coins in his pocket. Oh, hell! Couldn't go for a better cause.

"Sarge, we go right past the sutler's." He rattled the coins, "I owe you one."

Sarge was pleased to accept payment, not noting that he drank three to Mike's one. Neither did he notice that Mike staggered and leaned and finally upset the table where the cook had cooled the baking.

The Sergeant kept thinking about the cottonwood logs masquerading as cannons. "Give the general something to think about while dust gets in his eyes."

Mike Murphy picked up loaves of bread as he picked himself up. The loaves went through the window bars. He understood a small stir below as thanks and replied, "*De nada*, it is nothing," to the dark.

General Henry Hopkins Sibley, CSA, with about twenty-six hundred men had crossed the south end of the *Jornada*, threatening Fort Craig. For two days swirling dust pinned his forces down while patrols spied out the earthworks. The gun bastions at the corners made clear that direct assault would mean the loss of many lives. Nearly two thousand additional troops, largely California and New Mexico volunteers, worked to finish and strengthen the defenses of the fort. Since the corrals and stables, various offices and commissaries, quarters for troops and officers were backed up to the high earthen wall, the strength was doubled.

Wisely, General Sibley, CSA, decided to by-pass the fort. Since his aim was Fort Union, north of Albuquerque and Santa Fe, an attack on Fort Craig would mean unaffordable losses. The Confederates planned a stealthy by-pass hidden from sight of the fort by a swale on the east side of the river. A few miles up stream they would cross at Valverde. Colonel Thomas Green was chosen to lead the maneuver since General Sibley had become ill.

While the Confederate forces eyed the Federals across the river, the building of the earthworks, wall and ditch around the fort went on feverishly. Only the north central portion remained unfinished when the Federal patrols discovered activity readying for movement in the rebel camp.

Things became difficult for Private Murphy. The corrals, stables and the sutler's offices at the far end of the enclosure from the corner near the guardhouse where the work went on made it almost impossible to steal a bale of hay or a bundle of fodder for *los viejos*.

Juan Garcia fared little better. the cook at the guardhouse kitchen had grown suspicious and started counting the loaves at every baking. At times, when his low whistle brought Juan and *los viejos* to the wall under the window, Mike had only a handful of weevily hardtack to throw out to them.

The officers made uneasy neighbors too. Noisy they were. All over the place at all hours and not having enough to keep themselves busy. They were careless with candles and lanterns and, with the magazine which stored howitzer shells close by, Mike thought it was only a matter of time before they burned the place down or blew it up, whichever came first.

As Mike had feared, Captain Paddy Grayson caught Juan Garcia and *los viejos* huddled against the wall, all three too frightened to run had they been able.

Mike could do nothing, except maybe speak up hoping there was a drop of human kindness in the man. "Sir," saluting smartly, "Couldn't you just run them off? They look sick, *bueno por nada*, good for nothing."

"I may think of something." The Captain looked from Mike to *los viejos* and to the stack of boxes beside him. He grinned broadly. "I've been wondering how to send Sibley a going away present. Stay there – you've got the lingo – you and the Mexican can drive these old bags of bones."

Mike didn't understand as he watched the detail the Captain had called out. The men opened boxes of howitzer shells, then lashed a box on each side of the burros. The men laughed as the Captain explained. "We'll get as close as we can, then light the fuses," he jerked a thumb toward Mike and Juan, "they'll run the burros close, and we'll watch the fun. Bang! Bang! Bang!"

Mike shivered with horror. He knew what General Sibley's surprise was going to be and he could do nothing to prevent it. He watched helplessly as the patient starved beasts were readied for their death. He *had* to do something. They shouldn't go hungry.

"Sir," he said, hoping they would think he joined in the joke, "they're so starved they may not last. Could they be fed before we start?"

The Captain stared at Mike, then laughed ghoulishly. "The condemned ate a hearty breakfast. Why not?"

Mike ran into the guardhouse kitchen. Maybe something – the baking cooled on a table. The cook had just set out a pot of frijoles, the army's standard fare. Mike grabbed two empty molasses buckets, dumped them full of frijoles, poked a loaf of bread in each, pulled a handful of dish towels from a line and started back.

"Hey, you!" the cook started at the burglary in progress. "You're the blankety blank that's been lifting my bread!"

"Want to make something of it?" Mike growled over his armload.

The cook decided he didn't and Mike ran out. He knotted the dish towels into a fastening and using them for padding, hung the buckets of beans and bread around *los viejos* necks. The burros nuzzled him as he whistled softly to them, then plunged eager mouths into the food.

He patted the trusting heads, then broke off a chunk of bread for Juan. Muttering to himself, "The Captain's likely right, damn him!" he said sadly to them, "*Viene, amigos*."

Captain Grayson led the patrol silently to the river and through the chilly crossing. They skirted the restive hundreds of mules that pulled the supply wagons. Mike wondered why animals frantic for water were being held in a dry camp within sight and scent of the river, but supposed there was a reason.

Safely away from the sentries, Captain Grayson sent the patrol back and saw to the lighting of the fuses himself. "I set them fairly long," he said, "but don't waste any time. Follow long enough to be sure the burros are aimed straight at the tents," he said. "Then you get the hell out of there." He added not unkindly, "and don't look back. The poor little devils couldn't have lasted much longer anyway."

Then he trotted back to the detail waiting in the dark for the "fun." Mike and Juan let the burros draw ahead as they fearfully watched the spitting lines of the burning fuses.

"Do you reckon they've had time to empty the buckets?" Mike said. Then he turned to Juan, "Let's go." He looked at the moving lines of fire. "*Adios, los viejos*," he said with a short farewell whistle as they began running back.

Suddenly the swale where the Captain and the detail waited to watch the "fun" came to noisy life, shouting and retreating in headlong flight. Then a last look behind sent Mike and Juan running too.

The lines of sputtering fire that marked the fuses had turned and were coming back. Mike's farewell whistle had recalled *los viejos* to the only friends they knew.

Crashing and blundering through the swale, tripping and colliding with the *bosque* trees and reeds, the men had reached the river bank when the crashing explosions and shockwaves threw them into the water. Scraped and bleeding and bruised from falls and flounderings, and half-drowned besides, they had reached the western bank when the first wave of mules overran them.

The teams that pulled thirty of General Sibley's supply wagons, frightened by the exploding howitzer shells had burst out of their corral. Frantic with thirst, they stampeded to the river. Captain Grayson's men, Mike and Juan among them, dodging mules took to the water again. Swept through a churned-up river more mud than water by that time, they sprawled on the bank watching bobbing lanterns from the rebel camp advancing toward them.

Into the river again.

Private Murphy found the soldiers in the dark were the advance of Colonel Canby's column. Nearly the entire force of Fort Craig had marched to meet the Confederates at Valverde Crossing.

Not knowing the commander's strategy, Private Murphy found any battle confusing, but surely Valverde was the worst.

Morning came with neither Commander on the field at all times. Colonel Canby had not marched with the Fort Craig Federals. General Sibley came late in the morning but soon retreated to his ambulance. The Federals prevailed at first, but by mid-afternoon the initiative had shifted. Captain Alexander McRae's Union battery reeled from repeated attacks by the Confederates.

Captain McRae, wounded in the first charge, ignored pleas to surrender called to him by Confederate officers who had been his classmates at West Point. Instead, he asked for support from Federal regulars and New Mexico Volunteers commanded by famous Indian scout, Kit Carson. The combined Federal forces could not withstand repeated Confederate charges. Captain McRae was killed and the battery was captured.

The Confederates turned the battery upon the Fort Craig men and sent them back to the fort. Although General Sibley's troops won the day, they allowed the Federals to withdraw to the safety of Fort Craig without further engagement. Colonel Canby's superior force had lost the battle.

Private Murphy, swept back and forth as the battle waxed and waned, decided he had had enough of military life. He wasn't a deserter. If anyone cared to check him out, it would appear that his enlistment had expired two months since. He was a free man.

The rising moon silhouetted two peaks of the mountains that he had heard named the Rabbit's Ears. To erstwhile Private Murphy the peaks were more like burros' ears.

"*Por favor, Señor* – " the plaintive voice came from the huddled, muddy heap that had been flung to the river bank by the surge, then retreat of the battle.

"*Hombre*, is that you?" He knew that it was Juan Garcia even as he asked. At the same time he knew what Michael Murphy's future held for them both.

They had come to rest near the Confederate mule corrals in a welter of broken harness, rope, wagons, sheets, probably a tool or two if one looked closer, an ax and a shovel by preference. Shadowy forms moved among the wagons. Some of the General's mules had wandered back to the only place they knew. They could be hitched up with little trouble, he felt sure.

A team of army mules pulling a supply wagon driven by two unremarkable men, one a native and the other in a torn and wet uniform, could drive south and not be noticed. Living off the land might gaunt them a little, but rabbits were plentiful. If a native used to the land and an Irishman who could learn could not make a living in the green, fertile Mesilla Valley below Fort Selden, well Erin go braugh!

He looked up at the mountains where the beaks like burros' ears rose clearly against the rising moon. He though of two uncomplaining small creatures, serving and loyal. He stirred up Juan Garcia.

"*Viene, amigo, viene*," he said picking up a rope end.

Cramped and Crowded

Sergeant John Bennett, California Column volunteer stationed at Fort Cummings, New Mexico Territory, swore when he whacked his elbow as he finished his stint as postmaster.

When exaggerated care, he removed a single post card from the pigeon hole marked IN, placed it in the pigeon hole marked OUT, took it out and locked it in the mail bag ready to go to Florida Station on the newly arrived Atchison Topeka and Santa Fe rails. Now to get his detail riding.

He hit his elbow again and swore again. Within high adobe walls (rare in southwestern forts) one hundred officers and men, and sixty-five horses and mules were crowded together. As required "to furnish protection to travelers on the Butterfield Trail to California."

He would have elbow room as he led a detail to protect some swearing miners turned road builders. They were grading George Brook's steep, twisting wagon road through Hadley Draw at the Cooke's Peak mines. He thought with some disgust that road was just what civilians would do. Run a road right through an Apache *rancheria* then call out troops to protect them from their stupidity. In all honesty he had to admit there wasn't any other place the road could go.

The most valuable lead-producing area in New Mexico Territory depended upon that road. On it supplies were freighted up to the mines and the ore wagons thundered down. Now that the steel rails had reached Florida Station, making possible a junction with the Southern Pacific at Deming, the Cooke's Peak area ore could be profitably sent to El Paso for smelting. Profitable was the word, the Sergeant thought. An average of two or three railroad cars of lead carbonate a day mounted into real money.

Checking the detail – he had tapped Mulligan and Jones, Terrill and Clancy. Four were enough. They wouldn't have much to do – no patrol. Apaches hadn't been troublesome lately. This trip wasn't needed. He told himself to stop carping about the duty. The frontier, bulging from western expansion had broken to spill hundreds into the Territory. First stop the spring, that life essential in a desert land. Fort Cummings, established in 1863 (named to honor Major Joseph Cummings, poor soul, killed in ambush at Horseshoe Canyon two years earlier), had stood guard ever since. The discovery of lead on Cooke's Peak had brought hundreds of miners who needed to be protected from the Apaches who couldn't be expected to like being elbowed out of their own land.

"And that's where we come in," said Sergeant Bennett, checking the detail, "Mount . . . Ho!"

Traveling from the fort to the mines on the mountain meant a hot climb. The water resources on the nearly nine thousand-foot peak were meager. The one big spring, like the mountain, had been renamed to honor Lieutenant Colonel Philip St. George Cooke, Commander of the United States Army of the West's Mormon Battalion. (The Sergeant rolled all that out impressively.) The only sweet water spring high up the mountain yielded small amounts that were classed as luxuries.

George Riley, living near the spring, regularly filled small wooden casks with the cool sparkling water, loaded the casks on his burro pack train and then visited the mines. He had no trouble selling the entire supply carried by his Jackass Express.

With the detail dismounted and at ease, the Sergeant squinted hopefully up the slope, but he saw no movement. A tin cup of fresh cool water would be worth six-bits. That August day in 1879 was hotter than the hinges. He hoped Riley didn't sell out before he got to them.

He walked over to the nearest mine head. It might be the *Desdemona, Othello, Montezuma* or the *Graphic*. He couldn't tell – just that they had been staked out early, before his time. When the discovery strike was made, the more reckless miners dared the Apaches alone until Fort Cummings was reactivated. With some protection assured, the mines grew until three camps, Hadley, José, and Cooke's dotted the mountain slopes.

The Sergeant scuffed up a lump of the yellowish, honey-combed ore he had learned to recognize as lead carbonate rich in sixty to seventy percent lead with traces of silver after concentration. The early claims were shallow trenches; the veins lying almost on the surface. As the digs went deeper into tunnels, Sergeant Bennett had been told of fabulous clumps of pure metal caught in pockets the miners called 'sugs.'

Many of the digs were shallow so that heads popping up here and there made them resemble a prairie dog town, the Sergeant thought with a grin. Naturally curious, he struck up conversations with any miners who would talk.

"A mining expert you are!" he jeered at himself, but a man learned by asking questions and listening to the answers. He had learned not to be inquisitive with the older men who had gone down in the mines for a long time. They were often too cantankerous and grouchy to do more than swear at you. He thought there was some connection between temper and working in the tunnels for a long time.* It might rub off – he hurriedly dropped the lump of ore he had been turning over in his fingers. There was something the miners called Underground Sickness.

* The lead-rich ores, when handled for long periods of time, caused varying degrees of poisoning with serious physical and emotional symptoms and conditions.

The Jackass Express came into sight over a rise in the road just as a messenger on a lathered horse galloped in from the fort.

"Victorio's Apaches are out," he yelled. Dimly heard from the Fort came the dreaded long roll of drums that alerted all to danger, "Wiped out a family traveling this way!" Captain's orders; come inside the walls. Can't guarantee safety otherwise."

The Sergeant knew the drill. Two troopers he sent to Cooke's, two more to José and took Hadley for himself. Most of the women and kids were there. He knew he would have his work cut out getting the women and bundles and the babies rounded up and started for the fort – news of the massacre would put go in their heels but there were always one or two who wanted to wait to get the bread out of the oven or pick the washing off the line. They wouldn't tarry; women in this end of the Territory didn't dare the Apaches.

The miners were something else. The Sergeant puzzled over their seeming indifference to danger. True, every man jack believed he could take a war party all by himself but it was more than that. Too many men who had boasted got scalped. He had finally concluded their collective attitude was like a flock of birds when a hawk threatened. You'd expect each bird to get the hell out as fast as their wings could flap – buzz off in every direction. Instead, the flock closed in like a swarm of bees. The predator didn't dive into the whirling mass but waited for any unlucky bird who flew out and so became a target.

So he wouldn't worry too much about the miners but there weren't enough horses for the women and children. He made a quick decision. Start the bundles and the babies walking and riding whatever was available; fort up the pupils and teacher in the schoolhouse and wait for the troopers and whatever miners to come down. Then there should be enough horses to double up and catch up with the women. If Victorio wasn't too close – the Sergeant crossed himself.

The teacher was young and pretty and foolish. He was surprised to find school keeping in summer time but supposed whenever they could find a teacher they'd start up. He sternly ordered the school marm to lock up and keep the kids inside but ready. She wanted to argue. He was upsetting the children, she said, making them afraid when no one had seen any Indians.

He didn't take the time to tell her if she saw any Indians it would be too late. He snapped at her and when she indignantly went inside, he wedged the door and stood guard.

Keeping them shut up wasn't an answer. The schoolhouse was more of a tender box than a fort. If Victorio came – God forbid – one fire arrow would set it alight and roast everybody alive. With only two horses, his and the teacher's tied out back – and twenty-some kids, he could only pray and wait for the troopers and whatever miners to get here first.

With a splintering, the schoolhouse door burst open. The teacher stood in the doorway holding the poker that had done the damage. Glaring at him, she shouted angrily, "Soldier, you can't keep us cooped up any longer! The children are tired and thirst and some of them need," she stopped while trying to think of a genteel way to say it.

The Sergeant was crude. "Have them squat in a corner, one at a time, and you spread your skirt in front."

She stood red-faced and speechless, then went inside. He watched with a sinking heart. He daren't start the kids walking and there was no other place to fort up.

The Indians appeared as Indians do, rising up before your eyes, instantly filling a space that had been empty a second before. Three? Four? Dear God, let it be only a scouting party – but the strength would not be far away.

Behind him, he heard her gasp. "Keep the children inside," he ordered.

Again, he couldn't believe his eyes. A miracle! Like an answer to prayer, George Riley's Jackass Express plodded over

the small rise. At the thought of those casks of sparkling water the Sergeant's throat dried up like a sand dune.

Why had he felt any elation? Indians preferred mule meat to any other. The burros of the Jackass Express would draw them like bees to honey. He turned to see where the scouts were.

They had moved closer. The Sergeant thought he could see an awareness, almost an excitement at sight of easy prey. The sun silhouetted their single feathers, the hawk-like profile of their faces.

Feathers? Hawk? He danced on the doorstep, whistled and made imploring beckoning gestures. After a moment of puzzlement, George Riley got the message and whacked the burros out of their plod to a trot. The Sergeant whirled to face the girl, then pushed past her into the schoolroom to snatch up the broom, a water bucket, a feather duster and a bell from the desk.

"Don't ask questions!" he yelled at her. "Line the kids up at the door with anything they can find to wave," he reached in and plucked the calico curtain from the single window, "like this, or make a noise!" He clanged the bell, "Like this!"

He was back on the doorstep, poking the feather duster down his back to flaunt overhead. "Hand the kids to me, one at a time, then you nip out and get on your horse and do whatever comes to mind."

Riley and the first burro had reached the steps. "Circle the wagons!" he yelled at the startled man. "Take on boarders!"

It went like clockwork. She patted a child reassuringly, handed him to the Sergeant who plumped the kid into Riley's arms who, after one or two false starts, inserted the passenger among the nearly empty water casks. Then he moved the next burro up for the next child.

"Twenty kids; ten burros with twenty water casks; neat!" The Sergeant looked into the girl's eyes, kissed her smackingly and gave her a swat. "Run, darling! and pray!"

The burros trotted clockwise in a tight circle. The children among the water casks were dumb-scared or crying at first, then they began to yell and bang and batter with whatever was at hand. They waved jackets and shirts and long stockings. Teacher waved her skirt and rode shamelessly in white ruffled drawers. The Sergeant put his hat on his horse's head and whooped to put an Apache to shame.

When the children stopped crying and yelling, Teacher started them singing. George Riley, with the schoolhouse water bucket on his head, directed *The Battle Hymn of the Republic* with the broom.

The Sergeant caught sight of the transfixed Apaches and charged at them with the wildly ringing bell.

"*Loco! Loco! Muy loco*! Crazy!" he yelled. Plainly, the Indians couldn't agree more. They melted away with fearful glances over their shoulders.

In the exhausted silence, a first-grader began to cry, "Miss Teacher, I couldn't help it! I wet my pants."

"Who's going to pay for my spoiled water?" George Riley demanded.

The Sergeant bent to kiss Miss Teacher's hand that he held in both of his. The four troopers and a few miners from Cooke's and José came into sight at a gallop. They sent a few shots to hurry off the Indians, then turned the circling Jackass Express into a column headed toward the women with the bundles and the babies and the fort.

The Sergeant was so relieved he made a crude joke to answer George Riley's question. "Didn't you hear what the little guy said? He made water. You've got more than you had."

He looked at the school teacher fearfully. What would she think of him? The radiant smile she gave him overlooked the crudeness and expressed her relief. All of them were sure to be crowded together inside the walls of Fort Cummings like peas in a pod. The Sergeant thought, returning the teacher's smile, crowding wouldn't be so bad!

Halfway to the Guardhouse

Lieutenant James Haskell, 9th Cavalry, United States Army posted to Fort Selden, New Mexico Territory, knew he had only seconds to decide what to do –

Keep the Captain out!

He strode to the barracks door, avoiding the astonished stares of the troopers. If the Captain saw them sidling to close up the gap where Remus should be standing to inspection, the Lieutenant would be half-way to the guardhouse.

He stepped outside so the Captain could stop in the shade of the barracks to pat his forehead with the folded handkerchief in his hand. The New Mexico sun bore down on the morning. James Haskell hurried to get in the first word.

"Sir," said precisely and with an impeccable salute, "with the Captain's permission, I ran the bunk inspection. Didn't think you would mind, sir." He dropped his voice to add, "Mighty hot in there and not too sweet smelling."

The Captain was grateful. In the same low voice he said, "Thanks, Jim, I've got a head this morning."

The Lieutenant reported, "Bed and gear inspected, sir; men present," he crossed his fingers at his side, "and accounted for."

The Captain saluted. "Inspection report received. Dismissed."

He about-faced and went off to Headquarters. The Lieutenant swept the troopers with a stern stare that told them to hold their gab, and went away himself.

Needing an excuse to go after his missing trooper before too many noticed, the Lieutenant found it with the quartermaster who was longing for some green stuff to vary the monotony of beans and salt horse.* He quickly negotiated to borrow the team and buckboard the Captain's wife kept for family occasions. In town he could arrange for a wagon load of onions, tomatoes, potatoes, and anything else handy, to come as soon as possible and himself bring back the buckboard filled up.

Trotting briskly away from the fort, the Lieutenant decided to drop in at Leasburg. The bar and semi-hidden brothel there were off limits, but about the only place the troopers could reach. Should he find the missing Remus there, he wondered what he could do with him. Leave him out for the Apaches? Bring him in to be dealt with as a deserter?

Remus was a good man, some younger than most and too gentle for army life, but trying to find a place for himself in a world that had little place for a free man of color. The regiment, formed after the war under white officers, had offered opportunity to serve out west by building forts and fighting Indians.

At Leasburg, a questionable oasis with trees and a deep-flowing bend of the river, he made a loud announcement of his arrival and the settling of the team at the hitching rack. In the squalid bar and semi-hidden brothel smelling of rotgut whiskey and the girls' loud perfume, he nodded briefly to four or five civilians innocently drinking out of coffee cups at cleared poker tables. He ordered a bottle of soda pop, passed the time of day, and asked if Trooper Remus Jefferson had been there, or if anyone knew his whereabouts. Predictably, no one had seen him or even knew anyone by that name. So he headed for Las Cruces.

---

* The cavalry's name for corned beef.

As they trotted briskly, the Lieutenant talked to the team, who were his old friends. He found attentive listeners, ears pricked to catch his voice above the rattles and hoof beats.

"Let's talk about me," he said. "I've got problems too – not the same as Remus, but I'll have to be making up my mind before long." He stopped talking to grin at the memory his words had recalled of his Irish grandmother who couldn't tell what she thought until she saw what she said.

"You may not have heard," he told the horses, "but the fort is due to be deactivated pretty soon. Once we were slated for big things – General Sherman planned expansion for the fort, the nod went to Texas. Politics, surely, a lowly lieutenant like me wouldn't understand."

"So what about me? I like the Cavalry, especially working with you guys," he told his listeners, "and I like and respect my Buffalo Soldiers. I can be re-assigned with them, or listen to Liz." He explained, "You know, the girl I left behind? She wouldn't come out here to marry me and live at the backside of nowhere, but she can probably get her papa – he's a general – to find me a desk job in Washington – that is, if she still wants to marry me."

He thought about comparing the desert southwest with Virginia. He looked across the brown-bronze distance bordered by shining river and green valley, the mesa tilting upward to blue and purple peaks soaring against bright turquoise sky. He had become used to this country and no longer expected it to be like "back home." With surprised conviction he knew that this stark, beautiful country had become home!

He couldn't be quiet with the new revelation. He stood up in the buckboard and reached for the whip. Cracking it over the backs of the startled team, he yelled exuberantly.

"Let's have some action, boys! Come on, *git! Go!*"

He wasn't going to flick the team's shining hides with the snapping whiplash, and the horses knew he wasn't, but they obligingly lifted to a gallop and rattled down the rutted road, both man and mounts thoroughly enjoying the run.

When a fence and a mailbox and a tree came up at the side of the road, the Lieutenant turned out to give them room. The swerve threatened the trooper who had crouched concealed in the tall roadside grass. In a panic the man ran ahead of the rig, then crossed, barely escaping the flying hooves, to bring up against the fence. The girl who had come to open the mailbox stared at the trooper and he stared back.

The Lieutenant sawed on the reins and yelled over his shoulder at the trooper.

"Blast you. Halt! Halt, Remus! Nobody's going to hurt you. Stop!" Shock and surprise, rather than the command, rooted the trooper and the girl, giving the Lieutenant time to slow down and turn the team. Red-faced and sputtering, he snatched off his hat and searched for words.

The girl beat him to it. "The top of the morning to you, gentlemen," she said demurely, "Who shall I say has come to call?"

A pretty thing she was, the Lieutenant thought. Red hair tousled by the wind, bright blue eyes dancing with laughter, freckles across a turned-up nose – wouldn't most girls be screaming bloody murder?

"I'm sorry, miss," he began, "You needn't be frightened by Remus. He's a good man –"

Remus found his tongue. "Lieutenant, sir, if you could just look the other way, I'll make for the river, get out of sight. I won't go back, sir, I can't."

"I'm not going to take you back, you fool! I've risked my neck to find you, to get you someplace safe. Dammit, why did you run? Why didn't you come to me?"

"Sir, you couldn't have done a thing. Slannery bullied me once too many. I was cleaned up for inspection when I saw him in the corrals. I knew he was up to some devilment – like dirtying the fodder – but he outsmarted me. He jumped me, then knocked me into some horse hockey – excuse me, Miss."

"I hope you rubbed his face in it!"

"He's twice my size. I hit him a good lick with the shovel. After I knocked him into the water trough, I took off. Lieutenant, sir, he's after me all the time. I can't go back. I'd have to kill him one day."

"You're not going back, although the Lord knows what I'll do with you."

"There's men of color settled below Las Cruces. Maybe they'll let him mingle with them," the girl said.

The Lieutenant was impatient. "Walk all that way? Apaches would have his woolly scalp before daybreak."

The girl looked Remus up and down. "Ethan Brewster could use a good hand. We've got all sorts at Shalam. He wouldn't be noticeable."

The Lieutenant snapped his fingers. "That's where I've seen you before! When I came up from Las Cruces one time to pay my respects and maybe get some of the free love I'd heard you have – oh, sorry."

He hadn't stopped in time. She had to rise up on her tiptoes to reach him. Then she slapped him. Hard.

"Take shame to yourself, James Haskell!" she said fiercely. "Do you have to believe every dirty lie you hear? Go away! Don't speak to me!"

The Lieutenant carefully felt his cheek, wondering if a tooth rattled. She packed a real wallop.

"I most respectfully beg your pardon, Miss," he said humbly, "That was only what I heard. If you can excuse me? I'll need to stop by to see how Remus will be getting along. It will be hard to explain if you don't speak to me."

She kept her lips tight as she said, "I don't know if I'll want to speak to someone who believes everything he hears."

She looked at Remus sagging against the mailbox. "Straighten up, man! When I take you to Ethan Brewster, you'll have to look like you've got a day's work in you. Come on."

She looked over her shoulder at the Lieutenant. "I'll have to think about you."

He was almost certain her pretty mouth had the beginning of a smile. He thought about her all the way to Las Cruces and wondered how he could see her again.

The opportunity came surprisingly soon. When he bought all the fresh vegetables the general store had at hand, Henry Stoes, the proprietor, made a suggestion.

"Why don't you see if Shalam Colony will supply the fort? Ethan Brewster has planted every kind of vegetable I ever heard of – and some I never – hoping to market in El Paso. You could send a wagon down and I'm sure he would be glad to sell to you. Very glad, I'd think. Brewster has built hot beds and laid out big gardens that must have cost him a fortune. And besides, he pays half the men of Doña Ana a dollar a day wages."

"Makes a good-sized payroll," the Lieutenant said.

"Sure does." Henry Stoes was garrulous and not busy. "The bank sends it out every Friday, as everybody in the valley knows."

The Lieutenant's eyebrows lifted, and he whistled soundlessly.

"Exactly," said Stoes. "There's been one hijacking already, and there will be more or I miss my guess. The sheriff hasn't got the manpower for a guard, and besides, he's browned off at the Colonists. They won't prosecute if he catches the holdups. If they don't have enough spunk to take up for themselves, why should he worry?"

The storekeeper got back to business. "Let's have that voucher for the vegetables, young man." He reminded himself, "Say, how about some honey? The colony sent me two dozen combs today. It won't last long. Be a big treat for your Buffalo Soldiers."

The Lieutenant didn't have to think about it. "I'll take all you can spare." If the cooks baked hot biscuits to go with the honey, no one would miss Remus until too late to hunt for him.

At the fort the Captain lectured the troops and sent the Lieutenant out with a squad to make some token searches. The

Lieutenant, with the obvious approval of the troops, let Slannery know that, even though the thermometer registered 105 degrees in the non-existent shade, he was skating on thin ice. The name of Remus Jefferson was added to the deserters list and he was lost to public view.

It could have been observed that the Lieutenant found it necessary to go frequently into Las Cruces, returning by way of Shalam, since he needed to keep the supply of green stuff coming. Being very obliging, he did small errands cheerfully. On one round trip he went for a reel of cotton threat (J. and P. Coats #50) the Captain's wife needed. Since he was as ignorant of such matters as most menfolk, he took advice and instruction from Shannon O'Connell, the pretty Irish girl who had decided to talk to him despite his tendency to believe everything he was told.

One day when the Lieutenant arrived, half the colony had gathered at the mailbox and were buzzing like hives of honey bees. The bank payroll messenger – minus the payroll – sat on the ground holding a wet cloth against the side of his head. He was answering questions peevishly.

"No, I didn't see a thing or hear a thing either. Like I said, I was jogging along through the tall grass coming up to the tree and the gate – "

The Lieutenant interrupted the messenger, "Why didn't you stay on the road?"

"Wouldn't any fool want shade and grass instead of heat and dust? Like I said, I'm just jogging along, and next thing I know I'm flat on my back looking up at my horse who's looking down at me. And a lump on my head the size of an egg.

"That's it!" The messenger slapped his knee. "He was hid in the grass! Like an Apache! Or maybe he was one of them Buffalo Soldiers deserted from the fort. I was out cold, long enough for him to get away."

The Lieutenant glanced across the assembled heads and met Shannon O'Connell's gaze. "Hide in the grass? Apaches?

Buffalo Soldiers? No way!" He kept his face expressionless, but let one eyelid droop. She got the message.

Pushing to the messenger's side, she solicitously patted his shoulder and took the wet rag from his hand to refresh it in the pan of water. She stood to one side as she dipped and wrung. The Lieutenant could see no large lump or dark discoloration. When Shannon pressed the wet rag firmly on the spot, the messenger almost forgot to flinch.

The late afternoon quiet was broken by the soft clang of the bell calling them to the last meal of the day. Everyone would soon be inside.

The messenger visibly wilted, saying he must rest to regain enough strength to return to Las Cruces. He didn't want to make any trouble, he protested, he would just leave his horse here and slip away when he was able.

The Lieutenant and Shannon lagged behind as the others followed the bank messenger.

"He's up to something." Shannon was sure.

The Lieutenant asked himself, "What would be an average payroll? How much does a silver dollar weigh?"

Shannon responded, "That would be a *big* bundle."

Again their thoughts matched as they ran. "Near the tree!"

The Lieutenant lifted Shannon to the lowest branch. "Up you go!"

Then, enjoying a glimpse of long legs, he jumped to pull himself up beside her. They sat on their feet and hugged the tree trunk. In their hurry, if arms or legs were encircled rather than tree limbs, no one objected.

They were right in guessing that the stolen money would be hidden close to the tree to make sure no one would find it by accident. Soon the bank messenger hurried up, looking fearfully over his shoulder, bent and scraped in the tall grass.

Shannon whispered in the Lieutenant's ear, "What shall we do?"

His lips were close to her cheek. "Let him show us where it is – save us the trouble."

The messenger had utilized a hole at the base of the tree, then pushed dirt in to cover. "God bless that rodent." The Lieutenant's lips against Shannon's mouth were smiling.

The man scooped the fill with his hands and soon uncovered a canvas bag. When he gathered the bag in his arms, the Lieutenant yelled, "*Gotcha!*" He pushed Shannon and jumped himself.

Seconds later he helped the girl to her feet, made sure she was all right, and plucked the bag containing Shalam Colony's payroll from the inert messenger's grasp.

"He may never know what hit him," the Lieutenant said with some regret.

He gathered the girl into his other arm.

"As for you, young woman – "

"*Gotcha!*" Shannon whispered and kissed him.

* * *

Some weeks later the Lieutenant wiped his hot forehead and sat down on a nail keg to read the mail. He had worked hard all morning on his house, and he had the blisters to prove it.

He and Remus had laid up all the cured adobe bricks. The foundation and courses of bricks outlined one large room soon ready to roof. More rooms would be added when they had time.

"They!"

He quoted happily to himself: "Shannon O'Connell, late of Shalam Colony, and James Haskell, late of the 9th Cavalry, United States Army, are free to marry."

His request to be allowed to resign had been honored, but he would stay in the desert country he had come to love. He planned to invest every dollar he could find in Shalam's highly bred stock of horses and cows auctioned when the colony closed.

Too bad, James thought, for the colonists were good people, even if strange, who only wanted to save abandoned children.

He couldn't be too sorry. When the children were sent to other homes, Shannon, who had been one of Shalam's teachers, was free to may lucky, *lucky* James Haskell. He stared happily into the future.

Well, open the mail. His mother, bless her heart, urged him to begin wearing heavier undershirts for the weather was changeable at this season.

A reassuring letter from a friend in the Adjutant's office told him to keep his Buffalo Soldier out of sight until six months had passed, then take him in. Remus would be given a dishonorable discharge that would keep him from serving in the army again. Too bad, for he had been a good soldier, but he wouldn't have the fear of being charged with desertion hanging over his head.

A letter from his brother full of headquarters gossip he scanned until one paragraph leaped out at him. "The talk about Liz, the girl you left behind, is that she's been jilted by the lieutenant colonel she's been dancing with all year. You may be hearing from her. She asked me for your new address."

And there it was – addressed in Liz's stylish backhand. "She knew she had been a silly girl, but he would surely forgive her. It had just been an innocent flirtation with that egotistical mama's boy who had really *pursued* her. '... so, dearest James, if you urge me nicely, I'll come out to marry you. I would probably like ranch life more than the army, anyway ....'"

James Haskell groaned, then began to laugh. If Liz came, in spite of his failure "to urge her nicely," the meeting with Shannon O'Connell would be something to see.

Who Were the Savages?

Private Adam Tolliver, Company G, First Dragoons, stationed at Fort Stanton, New Mexico Territory, had been told twice in one day to keep his nose out of things that did not concern him. Not in so many words, but he got the message.

The first time he had been called "a bean-eater from Boston who didn't know the country." That was true. He wasn't used to miles of grass flowing over hills that crested in rocky mountains colored like Easter eggs, or green valleys fed by a thread of water called a river. Back home, such a little stream would be dismissed as a rill.

The second time he had innocently remarked that with all the empty country he could see, he had to wonder why the Indians were cooped up in *Bosque Redondo* Reservation at Fort Sumner. The gaunt, ragged men he had seen there didn't look dangerous.

Their cold and angry answers pelted him like hailstones.

"Ask any volunteer or army man if the Mescaleros are dangerous! They have been raiding and killing since 1855. Captain Henry Stanton, that this fort is named for, was killed right where you stand!"

" ... it took a bloody campaign to put the murdering lot where they can't raid and burn and kill any more."

" ... Uncle Sam feeds and clothes the lazy devils ...."

Private Tolliver decided to keep his nose out.

And so he did until the weather turned cold and his persistent cough worsened. His tour of duty in kitchen police was almost welcome for the stoves, kept fired up, made the kitchen warm and comforting.

Adam wasn't a *lunger*, at least he didn't think so, but his family's history of weak chests that frequently went on into consumption made him as careful of his health as he could manage. He stayed out of the wind and into the sunshine and got an extra blanket for his bunk. This high altitude and dry climate was said to be most healthful.

Proper food was difficult. Adam's mother admonished him in nearly every letter to eat eggs and drink milk every day, but both were in short supply at the fort. Beef and beans were more than monotonous.

Quality was worse than monotony. Adam got used to the weevily flour; you could sift it if you were squeamish. When the beef looked green and resisted a bayonet, the supply sergeant had one reply to complaints: "If you don't like it, don't eat it."

One day Adam couldn't stomach the look or smell of the chunks slapped to his mess kit. Making sure that cook was watching, he rushed to the door and slung kit and contents outside.

Almost before the tin hit the ground a stray dog darted at it. Then an Indian woman sprang at the dog, driving it away with a slashing stick. When the yelping animal drew back, the woman fell to her knees and fighting the dog away with one hand scrabbled in the dust for the food.

Adam stood transfixed. The cold, lifting, stinging sand plucked at the woman's ragged blanket exposing a cradle board strapped to her back. The sight even affected the cook who had come to the door preparing a tongue lashing for Adam.

"She had better get out of here fast," the cook said. "The Colonel has ordered all personnel to shoot any Indian off the reservation at *Bosque Grande*. The Agency has mixed up Navajos and Apaches there that are mortal enemies, trying to make them into farmers."

The Indian woman stood, pulling her blanket to best cover the baby in the cradle board. Adam saw that she was limping.

"You were right, Adam," the cook said. "That beef isn't fit to eat. That poor bitch must be starving." He turned to reach back into the kitchen. "Hell! She may as well have the rest of it."

He came out, having dumped the stew from the heavy iron pot into a lighter tin bucket. He called to the woman.

"Hey, Sister! Wait! Got something for you!"

She stopped, half concealed by a corner of the building and watched fearfully. As the cook went out, Adam ran into the mess hall to snatch up the heavy new blanket that had been folded to cushion a bench.

When they set bucket and blanket out they watched from the kitchen door. She waited for a long moment, then came out boldly.

With a petting motion she snugged the blanket over the cradle board, then around her own shoulders, pulling the warm wool over her head. She lifted the pail, then set it down to make a gesture of gratitude and thanks. Lifting the bucket with both hands, she disappeared as only Indians can.

"Kinda nice to know one squaw will sleep warm and full of government issue beef tonight," the cook said. He added, "You have to pay for that mess kit you threw out, Mr. Big Heart."

Adam couldn't forget the starved Indian woman. Actually, everything kept her in mind. A sentry shot a brave scavenging at the garbage dump. The Lieutenant searched for his missing dog; Adam never saw the stray again. If the Mescaleros were cooped up at *Bosque Grande* learning to be farmers and living at government expense who were these starving ghosts?

More to the point, where were those herds of six-hundred-pound cattle? Strange that they all weighed the same? Adam could ask those questions because he wrote a clear clerkly hand and was asked to copy forms and tallies and letters. He had to poke his nose further into something that was not his business. How to begin?

Off duty he walked down the road that led to Mescalero. The weather had turned cold and his persistent cough had worsened. He was hunting sunshine.

The man who had been sitting on a rock beside the trail stood up and said abruptly, "Soldier, turn your head to the right."

Adam did as he was told. The sunshine was warm on his cheek.

"Thought so when I heard that cough. Nice rosy cheeks, maybe stay a little warm? Sweat at night? Not the usual cheerful outlook, though." He smiled and held out his hand. "I'm a doctor, Michael Steck."

He saw that his name meant nothing to Adam. "I'm a salaried doctor, a civilian physician with the United States Army in the southwest. President Millard Fillmore appointed me Indian Agent for the Mescalero Apache tribe. Before long I was given supervision of all the agents."

"I've longed to talk to someone who could see both sides," Adam explained. "The Indians, sir, can you tell me what the hell goes on?"

"Greed! Greed, not only for money; greed for power."

The doctor shook his head. "You're a rare bird, soldier, if you can even see that there are two sides. That's what got me dismissed from the service. If you really want to hear?" he looked inquiringly at Adam, "it isn't a pretty story."

When Adam told him about the starving Indian woman, he could see he had found a sympathetic listener.

"One of my Mescaleros. Poor soul, trying to come home," the doctor said. "I'll keep it short. If you want the whole, official story you can look in the records. What it amounts to is the Indians wanted to keep their land as they had always lived on it and white men wanted the land without the Indians.

"After a lot of atrocities on both sides – there's blame enough to go around – somebody decided the only thing to do was round up the tribes, give them a reservation with a fort close by to keep them there. So far, so good."

Adam interrupted, "Sir, what about the starving and the greed?"

"You're a smart boy. You tell me what has happened."

Adam thought ahead of his speech. "A bunch of savages, that's what whites call red men, don't they, sir? plunked down on land not suitable, or big enough, or that nobody wanted, how could they live?"

"You're doing fine, son," the doctor said. "Go on."

"Until they learned to be settled farmers and ranchers," Adam interrupted himself, "that's asking them to change in a few years what we took thousands of years to become!"

The doctor nodded. "When weather and bugs and disease and lack of water make crop failures inevitable, agencies had to provide beef and beans, even some blankets." The doctor's grin was not one of amusement. "So behold a new industry is born! Supplying the reservations and their attendant forts under government contracts could make fortunes."

Adam made the connection. "Fortunes were made sooner if inferior food was delivered – or not delivered at all."

"Go ahead."

"Politics came into awarding the contracts and made enemies. When the hungry Indians raided their neighbors, the military oppressed them to keep the unsteady peace." Adam stopped. "How am I doing?"

"Very well considering that you are an outsider. I made the mistake of taking my charges' side and made some high-placed enemies. General James Carleton, no Indian lover himself, treated them so harshly I had to point out to Washington that it costs the government more than three million dollars a year to continue the practice of chastising and subjugating the Indians." The doctor shrugged. "I can't say the General's toes were the only ones I stepped on for I was asked to submit my resignation from the Indian Service."

In the long silence Adam could find no words to express his admiration and sympathy for the valiant doctor. Finally he asked, "What happens now? For you and for your Indians?"

The doctor shrugged. "I'll stick around. Look the other way. The general has given orders to shoot any Indian attempting to leave the *Bosque* Reservation. If they can get home to their mountains and hide out long enough, I think a reservation will be established in the Mescalero heartland. Then they will be called in."

"I am a soldier," Adam said, "what can I do? I have to obey orders." He dropped his head in his hands, then looked up miserably. "I can't just look the other way and do nothing."

They didn't hear the Indian. He was there in a space that had been empty. Ignoring Adam he spoke to Doctor Steck.

"Little Father, we cannot leave without your knowing. We will now go back to our mountains, everyone who is able to walk. Only the old and the sick will be left behind. We will return for them later. Our old men have counseled us. The soldiers can shoot one or two. How can they shoot a whole tribe? It is better that we go home to die than to starve here. We will never forget you, Little Father, and what you have done from your good heart."

Then the place where he had stood was empty.

Adam said wildly, "I am a soldier. I have to obey orders. I have sworn to do my duty. What can I *do*?"

The doctor stood up and started away. He said kindly, "I think you gave yourself some good advice. Just look the other way and say nothing."

The Value of Ingenuity

Sergeant Donovan Jones, known to the 82nd Battalion, USA as Dusty – due to an incident that marked his first days as a recruit – sat in the tall grass at the river's edge and focused his glasses on the Stanton Street bridge and the damn fools that crowded it and spilled out all the way to the Smelter.

The newspapers and the rumor mills had promised El Pasoans a bloody battle when the *insurrectos* attacked the city of Juarez and the crowd didn't intend to miss a single bullet that so far had whistled harmlessly over their fool heads. He swung the glasses to the hills where the rebels were camped, but he couldn't make out much activity. The rebels were throwing a few shells into the middle of the town, but Donovan thought his unit of horse-drawn artillery could do a better job if he were directing fire.

The word was that President Diaz was going to keep sitting on the boiling pot of rebellion believing he could keep on being *el presidente* as he had for about forty years. When everyone, particularly a noisy little rich man named Madero kept demanding silly reforms like free elections, Papa Diaz' solution was to jail Madero and ignore the growing numbers spoiling to fight for something or other.

Fort Bliss was under orders to stay within sound of the bugle and keep strictly neutral, but Donovan got into town often enough – when the wind was right you could hear the sound of the bugle a good long ways – to gawk at some of the foreigners who were willing to help for liberty or loot. He thought what *insurrectos* came over were a scroungy lot, but some were a little bit famous. Someone pointed out Garibaldi, grandson of the hero of the liberation of Italy, a writer fellow from New Mexico cowboys, and a real Dutch general who wouldn't live under British rule when his army was defeated in the Boer War in Africa. General Viejoen didn't look too much like a soldier but they said he was helping Madero with advice and his artillery. Donovan did see two who looked like soldiers: a tall gaunt man with fierce eyes named Orozco and a smaller fellow crisscrossed with bandoleers who were calmly eating ice cream sodas. Donovan saw that General Pancho Villa ordered a second soda and didn't pay for either one.

A short burst of small arms' fire must have been a signal. The bombardment began. Shells landed and burst in the center of the town. When Donovan saw that the targets were a safe distance from the river, he turned his glasses on the bridge. The damn fools had stampeded to the far end – Donovan thought he could see it shake – to stare avidly at puffs of smoke and clouds of dust. They had been promised a battle and, by God, they weren't going to miss it! They crowded back and forth on the bridge in a kind of ghoulish expectation.

Donovan thought he was as big a damn fool as the bunch on the bridge. The only difference was he knew how far a rifle bullet could carry and he was staying down stream where there was little to shoot at. Not to worry much for he guessed the rebels had old guns they had used to shoot rabbits, maybe backed up by bows and arrows.

To make him out a liar, a burst of fire sent up splashings in the river. Somebody would catch it for that. The rebels were surely short of ammunition. The gawkers on the bridge milled around in excitement but nothing more happened.

Donovan settled back in the grass. Like the other damn fools he was going to see a battle. He pulled some grass and chewed on the tender stems. Good forage, he thought – good horse country, too, by the look of it.

He admired the low interlocking hills furred with sun-cured grass that ran up to the mountains and down to the river. He liked this country the first time he saw it. When he had jumped down from the freight car in the El Paso yards and trotted a few steps to get his balance he had felt at home. He found where the fort lay, walked in and signed up, 82nd Field Artillery, 7th Cavalry, Horse-drawn.

He knew horses from childhood. He admired the trim business-like guns light enough for mobility (six horses to the limber) with enough firepower to make a difference. He hadn't been sorry in the two years since. He had made Sergeant and Section Chief and he liked it all. He had turned thirty last week and it had set him thinking. Did he want to live in barracks for the next twenty years? Lately he had been thinking he might like to settle down, own some land, maybe raise a family.

He had some money saved from pounding steel and setting sleepers on the railroads – only fools wasted hard earned dollars on gambling and girls – so maybe he could get hold of some land? Surely there was a God's plenty of empty miles out there. He could gather up a few 'stray' mama cows.

Donovan shook his head. He'd be an old man before natural increase (even if you helped nature along some) made him a rancher. Anyway he wasn't wanting to settle down with a bunch of cows. He wanted to get married.

He liked the looks of the Mexican girls he saw. Slim and graceful they were, big sparkling black eyes, great manes of hair, little hands and feet, and their talk like the chattering of birds. Even the ones who first went on the lines were like that, poor little devils. Donovan knew enough about life on the border to keep his distance from them.

He didn't see offhand how he could get to know any high-class girl. He'd observed that the upper-class Mexican papas guarded their girls more closely than they did their gold.

Donovan chewed on another grass stem. He decided he needed to find a Mexican papa who, first, had miles of land and more cows than he could tally, and, second, had at least seven beautiful daughters who needed husbands worthy of them. Donovan would be eligible for one or two. He had looked into enough pools of water to know his red curls and blue eyes, on top of six feet of Irish good nature, would interest most girls. So all he had to do was find the girl and con her papa.

He lifted his head to scan the river. Shells were landing in the town, where they mattered, not here on the border. His glasses picked up a few skulkers around the edges of houses, probably hiding out from the fighting around Federal fortifications. Some small stir by Chihuahuita. The girls over there were notoriously scrappy.

He lay back in the grass looking up at the cloudless blue sky and thought about a more immediate problem. How could he stay out of General Casner's way? Twice in one tour of duty was enough.

The first time he had been a brash recruit trying to avoid work, no different than any other layabout in the ranks. He had complained about the dust at the fort until his mates called him 'Dusty Donovan.' His worst gripe was having to give the extra pair of boots, required, under his bunk the required spit and polish job.

Then he had a bright idea. He varnished the extra pair.

At inspection the Brigadier had stopped in mid-stride. In the dimness of the barracks Donovan's boots shone like the rising sun.

"Hand me one of your boots, Trooper," the Inspector barked.

"Yes, sir!" he humbly said.

The Inspector turned the boot around in his hands, rubbed a finger and thumb over the slightly sticky surface and then handed it back.

"What's your name, Trooper?"

"Donovan Jones, sir."

"Very ingenuous, Jones," the Inspector said as he strode away.

Donovan had been 'Ingenuous' Jones to the whole Battalion ever since, but who would think he would draw the attention of (now) General Casner a second time? Yesterday he had started his three-month's training of a bunch of recruits shipped from back East who didn't know one end of a horse from another. He had begun by naming the parts of the animal and outlining the proper care and grooming. Then, fool that he was, he asked for questions.

The dumbest recruit of the bunch complained, "Sergeant, you give things such funny names—muzzle, crow, cannon, postern fetlock, dock. You expect us to remember all that? Like what's the dock?"

"You can remember that one," Donovan had snapped. "It's an ass hole like you! An ass hole like you!"

There was someone behind him. As he turned Donovan met the bland gaze of General Casner. The silence grew.

The General tapped his shining, dustless boots with his riding whip. "Still ingenuous, Sergeant Jones," he said, "but watch your language."

It was no consolation to Donovan that the General had remembered his name. Now all he had to do was keep out of the General's way for evermore.

Next day the border seethed with news. The *insurrectos* had stolen a train! They had stolen all the stock in the state of Chihuahua! The big rancheros had fled into El Paso, leaving all their wealth behind! The Battle of Juarez began! When stray bullets began to whistle overhead, the crowds on the river grew. This was what they had been promised. A battle!

Donovan worried. He got back to the river bank as soon as he could. He felt that things hung in the balance. American lives had been lost as the rebels came up to the city. The border was fragile. Was invasion unthinkable? Donovan told himself not to be foolish. No Mexican force, no glory-hungry general would *dare* to invade the United States!

Then the looting began. It was no longer a make-believe, almost a spectator, sport. The ragged, hungry soldiers could no longer be restrained. Smoke rose from burning houses. Those driven out, women and children among them, ran frantically toward the river and hoped-for escape.

Donovan's scanning glasses picked up two women running with a child dangling between them. Two soldiers emerged from a burning house, drunkenly smashed empty bottles against a wall, took aim and shot down the running women. They sauntered over to the fallen bodies and yanked up their skirts revealing one pair of ruffled drawers and one pair of blue jeans. Pleased that they had caught a male trying to escape in women's skirts, the soldiers staggered off leaving the crying child crouched beside the bodies.

Donovan cursed his helplessness. His rifle would carry that far but the murderers were inside another house and he could not invade Mexico as a one-man army. He scanned the river's edge up- and downstream; in case someone had reached that far, but saw nothing. The December low water level made fording possible in several places but any attempts would surely wait for darkness.

Something was moving from a screen of trees out of Chihuahuita – his glasses picked up a small buggy drawn by a small mule. He saw long black hair – a scarf tied around a head. Dear Lord, two women just asking to be shot!

While he held the glasses on the *rio* he saw a spurt from the surface of the water. The soldiers were shooting at the rig but not getting the range – yet. The buggy had come from Chihuahuita and two of the girls were trying to get away.

Halfway across the mule was in trouble. The water was only about knee deep but the buggy wheels were sinking. Another spurt of water from a closer shot. The mule strained against the harness but the wheels didn't move.

Donovan could stand it no longer. Those girls had as much right to reach safety as anyone, maybe more. This might be their only chance to escape to a better life.

He plunged into the river yelling at the two in the buggy. "Get out! Get out of the buggy! The mule can't pull you!"

He got a hand on the rear wheel when the mule went down in a splintering of shafts and tangling of harness. There was no time to see if he was hit. Everything shifted. The wheel went into a shallow hole, the woman with her head covered wrapped her arms around a leather covered small trunk and slid down to the end of the seat.

The black-haired girl spilled out into Donovan's arms. She clutched at him and for a moment she looked into his face. He saw the fear in her big eyes change to something else as his arms tightened around her. That something passed between them and Donovan knew he was never going to let her go – never.

The small woman, Donovan could see that she was older, had stopped urging the mule and with a stream of Spanish cracked the whip on Donovan's shoulders. In his astonishment, he let the filly slip from his grasp. She was little, too. The water came up to her waist.

"I don't know what she's saying, but you tell her she has to get out of here. Pronto! Whip and all!" He rubbed his stinging shoulders.

"She won't come. That's what she's saying."

Donovan stared at the girl who was weeping now.

"We came from El Paso to get them," the girl said. "She wouldn't rest when we got word that Ramon had made it up to Chihuahuita from the ranch."

Donovan's head swam but the cracking whip and the stream of furious Spanish decided him. He was wise in the ways of mules. He didn't see any blood stains in the water. If the load had been too much for him, which it plainly had been, like a sensible animal he had just laid down beside it.

"We have to move, mule or no mule," Donovan yelled. "Tell her!" He protected his shoulders from the cracking whip with his arms over his head.

"She won't budge," the girl wailed. "She says she'll shoot you if you try to make us go without them. She says," the stream of Spanish ended with something between a curse and a sob, "she says she has lost the cattle and the *casa* is burned and she isn't going to lose anything else."

Donovan saw that the fierce little woman did indeed have a pistol. He didn't doubt her determination to use it. He gave up. You couldn't fight a woman.

"What's your name, darlin'?" he asked the girl.

"Carita."

"Come on, Carita, we'll see what we can do before those rebels get the range."

Pablo wasn't shot. Donovan placed the girl at the mule's head with directions to hold on to the bridle – tightly – then he squirmed part way under the mule's hind quarters and began to twist his tail.

At the third twist, Pablo threw up his head and snorted. At the fourth, he got his feet untangled with a heave that threw Carita on his stomach. With a simultaneous snort, Pablo blew out the contents of that abused stomach in Donovan's face and scrambled to his hooves.

The fierce little woman allowed Donovan to carry her to ride facing backward on her precious mule. He saw that she could cover him that way while he went back for the leather covered trunk. It nearly drove him to his knees.

"What in the name of God do you have in here?" he demanded, staggering with its weight.

She didn't say.

It was easy after that. Donovan wadded his shirt into a pad that helped Pablo share the weight of the trunk and they splashed through the ford. The fierce little woman, riding backward, emptied her pistol at the soldiers on the Mexican side, and downed one.

Donovan saw they had drawn an appreciative audience from the Stanton Street bridge. He groaned as Carita wring out her skirts so she could walk. He could imagine what they were seeing. If he didn't get court martialled, he would never live this down. He looked fondly at the girl who looked at him with a smile full of promise. It was worth it all.

He heard a familiar voice then, but couldn't believe it. He stared at the immaculate figure coming to the river's edge.

"Good afternoon, Lieutenant Jones," the General said. "Ingenuous as ever, I'm glad to see."

Carita threw her arms around the General's neck and kissed him on both cheeks. "Oh *Abuelo* he saved us all. Isn't he wonderful!"

"Quite wonderful, as well as ingenuous," the General said. "I congratulate Lieutenant Jones on averting a possible international incident."

Donovan's head whirled, '*Abuelo?*' Grandfather? *Lieutenant* Jones? He knew the General could give battlefield promotion. Then he would be worthy of the girl who didn't come from Chihuahuaita after all. The beautiful girl who was certainly looking at him with favor.

Lieutenant Jones straightened up with pride in all his six feet. He had the girl. Rubbing the shoulder that *Abuela's* trunk had practically dislocated, Donovan thought that he probably had the gold, too.

Luck and Lightning

"Get the lead out, Lieutenant!" he told himself.

Then he grinned and revised his command. No more "Lieutenant James Haskell, 9th Cavalry, U.S.A. assigned for Fort Selden, Territory of New Mexico." Now just "Jim Haskell, civilian."

His discharge had come through. Fort Selden was being deactivated. He was free to stay in the Mesilla Valley that had become home.

From where he stood with the great river at his back, he looked across the valley, its burgeoning green muted to the bronze and tans of the mesa, then soaring like a blast of trumpets to purple spires against the sunshine. No, he wouldn't miss Virginia.

The Cavalry – yes. He patted the sawhorse beside him, probably the only mount he would know for some time. He hoped to bid on some of the fine Shalam livestock when the Colony dispersed soon. He told himself he had better forget horses until he got a start of mother cows. He hadn't decided whether he would become a rancher or a farmer. Probably cows were more practical. Shannon thought they could learn.

If he didn't get back to the adobe, she would call him a lazy layabout when she brought his dinner. He and Remus had laid up most of the cured adobe bricks. He had the blisters to prove it. The walls of his one-room house stood up almost ready for the roof. When *vegas* and *latillas* and a mud layer kept the weather off their heads, he and Shannon would get married. She wouldn't leave the Colony until the last child had been placed either in an orphanage or with a family. He knew how lucky he was that Shannon would marry him.

Whistling happily as he smeared mud-mortar on a brick, he wondered how he was going to get the roof on. Not a one-man job, that.

Still whistling, he lathered the adobe brick he held. Then, turning suddenly, threw the mud-smeared thing into the patch of tall grass and cottonwood sprouts beside the wall.

The figure that reared up held its muddy head and moaned. "You like to killed me, Lieutenant, sir! You didn't need to do that! I was just wantin' – "

"Come over here," James Haskell ordered. "Let me see who you are."

Furtive and hangdog, he recognized Trooper Slannery. What was he doing here? Then he knew.

"You're on the run," he charged the cringing man. "Why have you run here?"

"Lieutenant, sir, the troop's been sent way off somewheres. I just couldn't go – " The man gulped. "Sir, if you could hide me like you done Remus?"

So much for all his efforts to keep Remus out of sight. James Haskell, civilian wondered how close Lieutenant James Haskell, 9th Cavalry, U.S.A. had been to court martial. He told himself to be thankful for small blessings.

"Clean yourself up and find Remus at Shalam Colony. If he will let bygones be gone, you keep out of sight and do what you're told, hear me?"

"Yes, *sir*, Lieutenant, *sir*," the figure scurrying out of sight into the *bosque* said gratefully.

Whistling louder, Jim Haskell laid up another brick. He knew now how he was going to get the roof on his house.

The next two things happened at once. He felt like they had happened that way before.

As Shannon, bringing him dinner, came around the corner of the house wall, he heard the rattle of wheels, the thump of racing hooves – and surely that whoop was familiar? That female shriek?

Over the rise in the road, aimed straight for the mailbox, Pinkey's team and buckboard – "Mrs. MacArthur, Ma'am" – galloped, urged on by the standing, shirtless boy with hair streaming from under an Apache headband. He snapped a whip over the horses. A laughing trooper beside him held the boy up while Pinkey – "Mrs. MacArthur, Ma'am" – bounced on the back seat of the buckboard, wailing "Dougie! Dougie!"

When a back wheel uprooted the mailbox, the charge subsided in a cloud of dust. The cow who had been tied behind somewhere mooed plaintively. A *cow*?

The boy vaulted over a wheel and ran to James Haskell. A little taller now, he could pummel on a sweaty shirt rather than a yellow-striped uniform leg. The yelling was the same, just louder.

"I'm going to *get* you! Really *get* you! I'm still mad about my camel that you let get away! He was hungry and lonesome, and I wanted him for a pet!"

"Dougie, *Dougie*, I've *told* you over and over – " Pinkey, "Mrs. MacArthur, Ma'am," kept wailing and wasn't listened to. She seemed used to that.

James Haskell tried to catch and hold the pummeling fists. "Now listen to me, Dougie. *Listen*! Your papa wouldn't have let you keep the camel. If we could catch him – OUCH!"

The thump on his nose was painful. Wrathfully, James Haskell caught the boy in his arms. All the fight went out of Dougie. He clutched handfuls of sweaty shirt and leaned against the man's chest gulping and sniffing.

"It wasn't the camel – you were *gone*! Papa – and Mama, too – made me go to that sissy school – " Dougie gulped a sob and swiped fiercely at a tear. "When I came back the fort was moving! And you were *gone*. I didn't think I would ever see you again!"

The words ended in a wail. James Haskell hugged the boy and blinked away a tear of his own. Then Dougie straightened and pushed away with another grievance.

"I ought to *get you* for that too! My mama told you – I heard her! – you were supposed to take care of me. And you let them send me to that sissy school! And you were gone when I came back."

Shannon, who had watched them with a smile near tears, said loudly, "Hush your gab, boy! James Haskell is going to be right here. He will be a part of the landscape."

Dougie stared at her. "How do you know? – Oh, you're the Irish girl." His voice grew accusing. "I'm made at you too. You promised to tell me about those Irish fairy what-you-callems that turned into jack rabbits and burros. And you never did."

"You weren't here," Shannon said reasonable. "Now you are, we can talk all you please about the pookas." She changed the subject and pointed to Dougie's feet. "Those are great boots you're wearing."

Dougie admired them too. "When the guys laughed at my bare feet, I got tired of fighting. I'm used to wearing them now."

His mother clasped her hands and looked thankfully heavenward.

"So school wasn't all that bad?" Shannon asked.

"No." He thought about it, "They said I talked funny, but outside of that – "

The boy asked James Haskell anxiously, "It's true you have to go to school if you want to join the army? And be an officer? Like you and Papa?"

"Very true."

Dougie frowned, then decided,"I'll go then, but I don't have to like it. I reckon it'll make Mama feel better." He turned his frown on Shannon. "How come you know so much about what the Lieutenant will do?"

"I'm going to marry him. We're going to live here."

Dougie asked James Haskell anxiously, "Why do you want to get married? Is it all right with you?"

"Very much all right," James Haskell kept a straight face.

Dougie inspected Shannon at length. "Well ... I guess it's all right. If it's want you want, but it doesn't seem necessary." He asked James anxiously, "Can I come to visit? Will she let me?"

"Of course I will," Shannon told Dougie. "Any time. What makes you think I wouldn't?"

"Women are kind of bossy. They keep trying to make a guy over. Like that school wanted to tell me how to talk, said I sounded different, mostly I don't say big words, I guess. We have to go, but I'll be back." He laughed. "That school will have me saying it fancy – 'I shall return!'"

James Haskell wondered why Dougie's words sounded prophetic. Time would tell.

Pinkey – "Mrs. MacArthur, Ma'am" – interrupted the solemnity. "Dougie, your Papa is waiting to put us on the train at Las Cruces. Tell the Lieutenant and Miss Shannon good-bye now and explain about the livestock."

"I guess we have to go," Dougie was reluctant. "Moo Cow is a present from Mama and me, and you and Miss Irish can come along to drive the team back."

James Haskell rubbed his eyes and wanted to thump his head to clear things up. "A cow for a present? Drive the team back?"

"Oh, that," Dougie said, "We want you to have the cow. Papa balked at paying the freight on her. And the team's yours if I can drive it all the way to Las Cruces. Is it a deal?"

James Haskell felt doubtful. "I can scrape up enough cash to pay for the cow, but the team and the buckboard? No way, and what about the trooper?"

"He's kind of left over," Dougie said. "You can put him to work or take him someplace. And don't worry, you've paid for the team."

Haskell felt his mouth hanging open. "Paid? How?"

"Come on, Mama, Miss Irish – " Dougie put the ladies in the back seat. "You *promised* I can drive all the way to Las Cruces," he said to James. "I'm glad you will have the team. Papa's kind of mad about it, but he can't let it get out after all he's said against gambling. Remember that ten-peso note you wanted to bet on the Camel? And I took it away from you? Well, I mailed it like your letter said, and you won the Louisiana Lottery. Neat, huh?"

James Haskell braced the boy standing on the buckboard seat. As the whip cracked above the backs of the team – *his team* – and Dougie urged the horses to a gallop, they rattled and stormed down the rutted road. He hoped the wheels would take it.

James Haskell, late of the 9th Cavalry, U.S. Army, stationed at Fort Selden, Territory of New Mexico, yelled along with his reckless driver.

It felt wonderful to get struck by lightning.

BIBLIOGRAPHY

Fact and fancy mingle in New Mexico Territorial history. As vivid and varied as the personalities who lived them are the tales that may be found in these additional references.

L. P.

Mesilla Valley

Billington, Monroe Lee. *Buffalo Soldiers, 1866-1900*, Boulder: University of Colorado Press.

Howland, Jone. "Shalam: Fact versus Fiction," *New Mexico Historical Review*, Vol. 29, 1945.

Kelleher, Julia. "Land of Shalam: Utopia in New Mexico," *New Mexico Historical Review*, Vol. 19, 1980.

Priestley, Lee. *Shalam: Utopia on the Rio Grande*, El Paso: Texas Western Press, 1988.

Wiley, Elnora W. *Inside the Shalam Colony*, Los Alamos, NM: The Document Shop, 1990.

Fort Craig

Ryan, Andrew. *News From Fort Craig*, Santa Fe, NM: Stage Coach Press, 1966.

Staley, F. *Pampa*, Pampa, TX: Texas Print Shop, 1961.

Fort Cummings

Myers, Lee. "Military Establishments in SW New Mexico," *new Mexico Historical Review*, Vol. 43, 1968.

Parker, W. T. *Annals of Old Fort Cummings*, published by author, North Hampton, MA. 1916.

Fort Fillmore

Armstrong, A. F. H. "The Case of Major Isaac Lynde," *New Mexico Historical Review*, Vol. 36, 1961.

Narrative of a Surrender of U.S. Forces at Fort Fillmore, Santa Fe, NM: Stage Coach Press, 1960.

Stanley, F. *Fort Fillmore Story*, Pamap, TX: Pantex Print Shop, 1961.

Fort Selden

Cohrs, Timothy. *Fort Selden, New Mexico*, Santa Fe: Museum of New Mexico Press, 1974.

Milton, Hugh M., II. *Fort Selden, Territory of New Mexico*, Las Cruces, NM: published by author, 1971.

Fort Stanton

Stanley, F. *Fort Stanton*, Pampa, TX: Pantex Print Shop, 1964.

Wallace, Andrew. "Duty in the District of N.M.: Miilitary Memoirs," *New Mexico Historical Review*, Vol. 50, 1975.

Fort Sumner

Amaden, Charles. "Navajo Exiles at Bosque Redondo," *New Mexico Historical Review*, Vol. 8, 1933.

McNett, Franklin. "Fort Sumner: A Study in Origins," *New Mexico Historical Review*, Vol. 45, 1970.

Index